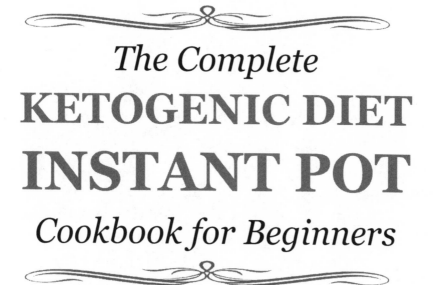

The Complete
KETOGENIC DIET
INSTANT POT
Cookbook for Beginners

PETER BRAGG

Legal & Disclaimer

The information contained in this book and its contents is not designed to replace or take the place of any form of medical or professional advice; and is not meant to replace the need for independent medical, financial, legal or other professional advice or services, as may be required. The content and information in this book has been provided for educational and entertainment purposes only.

The content and information contained in this book has been compiled from sources deemed reliable, and it is accurate to the best of the Author's knowledge, information and belief. However, the Author cannot guarantee its accuracy and validity and cannot be held liable for any errors and/or omissions. Further, changes are periodically made to this book as and when needed. Where appropriate and/or necessary, you must consult a professional (including but not limited to your doctor, attorney, financial advisor or such other professional advisor) before using any of the suggested remedies, techniques, or information in this book.

Upon using the contents and information contained in this book, you agree to hold harmless the Author from and against any damages, costs, and expenses, including any legal fees potentially resulting from the application of any of the information provided by this book. This disclaimer applies to any loss, damages or injury caused by the use and application, whether directly or indirectly, of any advice or information presented, whether for breach of contract, tort, negligence, personal injury, criminal intent, or under any other cause of action.

You agree to accept all risks of using the information presented inside this book.

You agree that by continuing to read this book, where appropriate and/or necessary, you shall consult a professional (including but not limited to your doctor, attorney, or financial advisor or such other advisor as needed) before using any of the suggested remedies, techniques, or information in this book.

Table of Contents

SOUP & STEWS   *91*

Book Description

That burning sensation in your chest after climbing up two flights of stairs, jeans that don't fit, or friends that tell you "I think you're getting chubby,"— are you getting a bit tired of this sort of thing happening? Are you anxious to lose those excess pounds you had carried around since Thanksgiving three years ago?

A Ketogenic diet is one of the best things that you could do for yourself! Trust me! Millions of people all around the world have already discovered this unique lifestyle.

Maybe you've already tried some of the fad diets that are popular right now, but they do not seem to work. Or maybe you have tried some of the fasting and starvation diets out there that promise instant results, but you are enthusiastic about the idea of skipping meals. Well, maybe it's time that you try a diet that is scientifically proven to help you burn fat, lose weight, and provide you with positive results beyond what you have considered - the Ketogenic Diet.

Also called as the Keto Diet, this food program is a low-carb high-fat diet that "forces" the body to enter into a different metabolic state where fat is burned as fuel for energy instead of glucose.

You may think that the Keto Diet is a relatively new food regimen, but this diet was once popular in the 1940's when it was used to help minimize seizures of children with epilepsy.

When anticonvulsant drugs became more widely available to the market, the diet's popularity faded as it was not necessary to combat seizures anymore. It only gained popularity again in the 1990's, when the son of a famous Hollywood director used the diet to help him reduce his epileptic episodes, with remarkable results.

This paved the way for further research into the Keto Diet. These studies found that a low-carb, high-fat diet was not only able to help minimize seizures for patients with epilepsy, but also help individuals to lose weight, reduce abdominal fat, increase HDL and LDL levels (good cholesterol), decrease blood sugar levels, prevent cancer, and cognitive decline. So in short, this diet that I am about to introduce you to, will not only help you burn fat and lose weight, but it can also deliver other amazing benefits for your overall health!

Embracing a Ketogenic diet will make you change your life for the better! It brings with it so many health benefits that are associated with this kind of food, which in turn makes feel amazing.

This diet is easy to follow, and it quickly yields results for those who adhere to it.

If you decided to start a Ketogenic diet, you should probably keep in mind some simple rules you need to follow!

So, have you started a Ketogenic diet yet?

Perfect! Then, all you need now is to learn how to make the best Ketogenic dishes!

There are endless amounts of Ketogenic recipes, and they are very unusual. In this book, we concentrate on a new way to prepare the keto meals: using a very advanced kitchen appliance – the Instant Pot! Begin your healthy life today.

Introduction

This book is a simple guide for the easy understanding of the Ketogenic diet, as well as a structured manual detailing the many ways one can use an Instant Pot to capitalize on this incredible lifestyle change.

The Ketogenic diet has revolutionized weight loss, providing millions of individuals with a new way to burn their fat stores for fuel, while reversing insulin resistance and pre-diabetes, preserving muscle, improving health, and boosting cognitive function.

A new trend among people who eat healthily and enjoy cooking with minimal mess and time is the Instant Pot. This type of cooking instrument has been around for several decades, but new models have come to the market vastly improved, and with health and convenience in mind.

In addition to pressure cooking, the Instant Pot can be used as a slow cooker, rice cooker, stove, steamer, and sauté pan.

There's no need to spend hours in the kitchen, standing over multiple pots and pans.

Simply choose a recipe from this book, pop in the ingredients, and come home to a hot, steaming meal that stays within the macro ratios of the Ketogenic diet by keeping meals low carb, high fat, and moderate protein.

The Instant Pot has become the favorite cooking tool for keto-enthusiasts everywhere, providing them with a "set it and forget it" way to come home to a healthy meal that ensures they keep using their fat for fuel instead of running on glucose and sugar.

At the completion of this book, you will be in an excellent position to start cooking the different recipes and begin living a ketogenic lifestyle!

Benefits of Keto Diet

The list of health benefits secured from a Keto Diet will never be ending. Nevertheless, for your convenience, a few of the more significant health benefits that you can gain from a Keto Diet will be explained.

- **Epilepsy**: Since Ketogenic diet is a diet that features high fat, low carbohydrate, and controlled consumption of protein, it causes the body to use fat as the primary energy source energy. In a lot of epileptic cases, switching to a Ketogenic diet has resulted in a lowered incidence of seizures. Exercise care and supervision when children are following the diet.

- **Reversing Type 2 Diabetes**: This is one of the benefits of being on a Ketogenic diet. There are many success stories about this diet, which research has proven is a result of lowering the amount of carbohydrate that you consume, and as a result, your blood sugar level is brought to natural homeostasis. It is important to note that carb stimulates the body system to discharge the hormone called insulin. So, when carb intake is lowered, the body does not release more insulin to control the blood sugar which will, in turn, increase the burning of fat that has been stored in the body. How then does this work in reversing Type 2 diabetes?

The answer to the question is simple. The fundamental problem faced by people with diabetes is a high amount of blood sugar that comes primarily from carb intake.

Once a person in on a Ketogenic diet, since they eat a fewer amount of carbs, the body can easily control the amount of blood sugar which has the capacity of reversing Type 2 diabetes.

- **Weight Loss**: What happens during ketosis? Your body shifts from burning carbs as fuel into burning fat which results in tremendous weight loss. As you dive deeper into the sea of ketosis, your body burns fat resulting in weight loss. Instead of other types of diets which may have been using for weight loss without success, with Ketogenic diet, you lose body fat and weight quickly.

- **Useful Mental Agility**: When ketosis mode is fully activated, there is a constant supply of ketones to the brain. Remember that when the body is not in ketosis mode and carb is steadily fed into the body system, the brain makes use of carb as a fuel source and many are of the opinion that to increase mental agility and focus, more carbs need to be consumed. On the contrary, when you are entirely in ketosis, your body registers a massive change in fuel consumption, meaning it burns more fat rather than the conventional carbs, resulting in fat in your body are broken down into ketone bodies. Other organs in the body can make use of fat. However, the brain makes use of ketones broken down from fat. During ketosis, there is usually an increase in the flow of ketone bodies to the brain giving it a more active mental agility and focus.

- **Acne Reduction**: It has been reported with the colossal success that many people who have acne problems when on low carb diets like the Ketogenic diet, their acne is drastically reduced. When on a Ketogenic diet the intake of carb is lowered. Where carbs are consumed, the body needs to produce the hormone called insulin to reduce the amount of blood sugar in the bloodstream. Acne is mostly caused and driven by insulin. It is the cornerstone of acne. Besides acting as the primary agent that motivate skin cells to manufacture sebum (an oily secretion secreted by the sebaceous gland for lubricating the hair and skin and protects against bacteria) and keratin (a fibrous insoluble protein that is the primary structural element in hair and nail), it heightens the secretion of many other hormones that causes acne. What does this all mean? When you are on a low carb diet like the Ketogenic diet, the flow of insulin to lower the amount of blood sugar in your bloodstream is not necessarily needed since your body does not require that.

Insulin, being one of the leading causes of acne, will be curtailed since you do not consume many carbs that will summon its presence in your bloodstream. When there is no sugar to reduce in the blood, your insulin will not be used as often.

- **Enhanced Stamina**: While practicing the Ketogenic diet, your physical stamina and endurance will be improved since you will have access to storage of fat that your body has reserved.

  At a time of intense exercise, your stored carbs will melt away like the dissolving ice beaten down upon by summer light. On the other hand, your fat storage can last longer than your carbs. When you are carb adapted, your fat stores are quickly depleted during a short time of intense exercise and to refill; you must keep eating. However, when you are on a Ketogenic diet, most of the fuel that is available is fat, with more long-lasting effects than your regular carb stores. Your body and your brain are energized by your fat stores making you last longer in exercise and have more stamina than someone who is relying on carbs for their strength and endurance.

- **Enhanced Performance**: Since your body is experiencing a shift from what it is used to, it is possible that at the formative stage of the Ketogenic diet you might experience some form of reduced performance.

But will this remain for a long time? Certainly not. The benefits of going Ketogenic are more long term than short term. Today many athletes are going Ketogenic, and they have improved their performance, especially in long distance running. As I have explained earlier, your fat stores last longer than your carb stores. Since fat stores last longer, an athlete can perform for a prolonged period without refueling with external energy.

- **Decreased Aging**: With the Ketogenic diet, your body can and will look younger for longer. When you have entered ketosis, ketone bodies are produced.

These bodies may decrease the aging process by blocking a group of enzymes known as histone deacetylases.

The enzymes function to keep a couple of genes known as Forkhead box O3 and Metallothionein 2A turned off.

These genes can empower other cells to resist oxidative stress. The good thing is that the ketone bodies produce when full fledge ketosis has been entered can block Forkhead box O3 allowing the genes to be reactivated which prevents oxidative stress because it is this oxidative stress that indirectly causes aging.

Besides, the Ketogenic diet reduces blood sugar levels.

It is important to know that when sugar levels are reduced, glycation and the production of enhanced glycation by-product materials made from high blood sugar heightens tissue damage, diabetes, and aging. Finally, the Ketogenic diet is a catalyst that reduces triglycerides which are known for causing a lot of terminal diseases.

- **Alzheimer disease**: This is a mental disorder that causes dementia because of the progressive degradation of the brain. One of the features of this disease is a decreasing ability to metabolize glucose. Whenever the mind is unable to metabolize glucose, it can have a lot of adverse effects on the brain. However, with ketone bodies when a person is entirely into ketosis, the supply of ketones to the brain reduces the brain's over-dependence on glucose.

Breakfast Recipes

Sausage and Cheddar Frittata

Servings: 4

Ingredients:

- ½ c. Ground Sausage
- ¼ c. Grated Cheddar Cheese
- 4 Eggs
- 2 tbsps. Sour Cream
- 1 tbsp. Butter
- ¼ tsp. Salt
- ¼ tsp. Pepper
- 1½ c. Water

Directions:

1. Pour the water into your Instant Pot and lower the rack.
2. Grease a baking dish that can fit inside the Instant Pot with some cooking spray.
3. Whisk together the eggs and sour cream, in a bowl.
4. Stir in the remaining ingredients.
5. Pour the mixture into the prepared baking dish.
6. Place the dish on the rack and close the lid.
7. Cook on LOW pressure for 17 minutes.
8. Do a quick pressure release.
9. Serve and enjoy!

Nutritional Info: 282 Calories, 12g fat, 1g net carbs, 24g protein

No-Crust Tomato & Spinach Quiche

Servings: 6

Ingredients:

- 1 c. Diced Tomatoes
- 3 c. Chopped Spinach
- ¼ c. Grated Parmesan Cheese
- ½ c. Milk
- 3 Green Onions
- 12 Eggs
- ½ Sliced tomato
- ½ tsp. Garlic Salt
- ¼ tsp. Pepper
- 1½ c. Water

Directions:

1. Pour the water into the Instant Pot.
2. Grease a baking dish with cooking spray.
3. Combine the diced tomatoes, green onions, and spinach, in it.
4. Beat the eggs along with the milk, salt, and pepper.
5. Pour this mixture over the spinach and tomatoes.
6. Sprinkle with parmesan cheese and top with tomato slices.
7. Place the baking dish on the rack and close the lid.
8. Cook on HIGH for 20 minutes.
9. Wait 10 minutes before releasing the pressure quickly.
10. Serve and enjoy!

Nutritional Info: 178 Calories, 11.2g fat, 3.8g carbs, 15.3g protein

Pepper Jack and Cheese Egg Muffins

Servings: 8

Ingredients:

- ¼ c. Shredded Pepper Jack Cheese
- 4 Bacon Slices
- 4 Eggs
- 1 Green Onion
- Garlic Powder
- Pepper
- ¼ tsp. Salt
- 1½ c. Water

Directions:

1. Set your Instant Pot to SAUTE.
2. Cook the bacon until crispy (for a few minutes).
3. Wipe off the bacon grease, pour the water inside, and lower the rack.
4. Beat the eggs along with the pepper, garlic powder, and salt.
5. Crumble the bacon and add to this mixture.
6. Stir in the onion and cheese.
7. Pour this mixture into 4 silicone muffin cups.
8. Arrange them on the rack and close the lid.
9. Cook on HIGH for 8 minutes.
10. Wait 2 minutes before releasing the pressure quickly.
11. Serve and enjoy!

Nutritional Info: 282 Calories, 12 fat, 1g carbs, 24g protein

Eggs and Cream

Servings: 4

Ingredients:

- 4 Eggs
- 1½ tbsps. Chives
- 4 tbsps. Cream
- Salt
- Pepper
- 1 ½ c. Water

Directions:

1. Pour the water into your Instant Pot.
2. Grease 4 ramekins with some cooking spray.
3. Pour a tablespoon of cream inside each ramekin.
4. Crack an egg into each ramekin, and make sure not to break the yolk.
5. Season with salt and pepper.
6. Sprinkle with chives.
7. Arrange the ramekins on the rack inside the IP, and close the lid.
8. Cook on MANUAL for 2 minutes.
9. Release the pressure quickly.
10. Serve and enjoy!

Nutritional Info: 173 calories, 16.6g fat, 0.8g carbs, 5.8g protein

Cheesy Chili Mexican Frittata

Servings: 4

Ingredients:

- 4 Eggs
- 1 c. Shredded Mexican Blend Cheese
- 10 oz. Chopped Green Chilies
- ¼ c. Chopped Cilantro
- 1 c. Half and Half
- ½ tsp. Cumin
- ½ tsp. Salt
- ¼ tsp. Pepper
- 2 c. Water

Directions:

1. Pour the water into the IP and lower the rack.
2. Beat together the eggs salt, cumin, half and half, and ½ of the cheese, in a bowl.
3. Stir in the chilies and cilantro.
4. Grease a baking dish and pour the egg mixture into it.
5. Cover the dish with foil and place in the Instant Pot.
6. Cook for 20 minutes at HIGH.
7. Wait 10 minutes before releasing the pressure naturally.
8. Sprinkle with the remaining cheese and cook for 2 more minutes on HIGH, uncovered.
9. Serve and enjoy!

Nutritional Info: 257 Calories, 19g fat, 5g carbs, 14g protein

Carrot and Pecan Muffins

Servings: 8

Ingredients:

- ½ c. Chopped Pecans
- 1 c. Almond Flour
- 3 Eggs
- ¼ c. Coconut Oil
- 1 tsp. Baking Powder
- 1/3 c. Truvia
- 1 c. Shredded Carrots
- 1 tsp. Apple Pie Spice
- ½ c. Heavy Cream
- 1½ c. Water

Directions:

1. Pour the water into your Instant Pot and lower the rack.
2. Place all of the ingredients, except the carrots and pecans, in a mixing bowl.
3. Mix with an electric mixer until fluffy.
4. Fold in the pecans and carrots.
5. Divide the mixture between 8 silicone muffin cups.
6. Arrange on the rack and close the lid.
7. Cook on MANUAL for 15-20 minutes.
8. Do a quick pressure release.
9. Serve and enjoy!

Nutritional Info: 263 Calories, 25g Fat, 4g Carbs, 6g protein

Smoked Paprika Eggs

Servings: 6

Ingredients:

- ½ tsp. Smoked Paprika
- 6 Eggs
- ¼ tsp. Salt
- Pepper
- 1½ c. Water

Directions:

1. Pour the water into your Instant Pot.
2. Crack the eggs into a baking dish, not breaking the yolks.
3. Cover the dish with foil and place on the rack.
4. Close the lid and cook on HIGH for 4 minutes.
5. Release the pressure quickly and remove the 'loaf' of eggs.
6. Place on a cutting board and dice the eggs finely.
7. Stir in the spices.
8. Serve and enjoy!

Nutritional Info: 62 Calories, 4g Fat, 0g Carbs, 5g Protein

Jalapeno Egg Poppers

Servings: 6

Ingredients:

- 6 Eggs
- 1 c. Shredded Cheddar Cheese
- 4 Jalapeno Peppers
- 1 tsp. Lemon Pepper Seasoning
- ¼ tsp. Garlic Powder
- 1 ½ c. Water

Directions:

1. Pour the water into the IP and lower the rack.
2. Beat the eggs with the garlic powder and lemon pepper seasoning.
3. Stir in the cheese and jalapenos.
4. Divide the mixture between 6 jars.
5. Seal the lids and place the jars on the rack.
6. Close the lid and cook on MANUAL for 8 minutes.
7. Release the pressure naturally, for 10 minutes.
8. Serve and enjoy!

Nutritional Info: 219 Calories, 16g fat, 2g Carbs, 18g Protein

Breakfast Almond and Coconut Cake

Servings: 8

Ingredients:

- ½ c. Heavy Cream
- 2 Eggs
- ¼ c. Melted butter
- 1/3 c. Truvia
- 1 c. Almond Flour
- 1 tsp. Baking Powder
- ½ c. Shredded Coconut
- 1 tsp. Apple Pie Spice
- Sea Salt
- 2 c. Water

Directions:

1. In one bowl, mix dry ingredients including the coconut.
2. Whisk together the wet ones in another.
3. Fold the two mixtures gently.
4. Grease a 6-inch round pan and pour the batter into it and cover with a foil.
5. Pour the water into your IP and lower the rack.
6. Place the cake on the rack and close the lid.
7. Cook on HIGH for 40 minutes.
8. Release the pressure for 5 minutes.
9. Serve and enjoy!

Nutritional Info: 236 Calories, 23g fat, 3g carbs, 5g protein

Sausage and Bacon Omelet

Servings: 6

Ingredients:

- 6 Eggs
- 6 Bacon Slices
- 6 Sliced Sausage Links
- 1 Diced onion
- ½ Milk
- ¼ tsp. Garlic Powder
- ¼ tsp. Salt
- ¼ tsp. Pepper
- 1½ c. Water

Directions:

1. Pour the water into your Instant Pot and lower the rack.
2. Beat the eggs along with the milk and seasonings.
3. Stir in the remaining ingredients.
4. Grease a baking dish with cooking spray.
5. Pour the egg mixture into it.
6. Place the dish on the rack and close the lid.
7. Cook on MANUAL for 25 minutes.
8. Release the pressure naturally.
9. Serve and enjoy!

Nutritional Info: 222 calories, 15.5g fat, 3.5g carbs, 16.8g protein

Egg Casserole

Servings: 4

Ingredients

- 2 c. water
- 1 chopped yellow onion
- 1½ c. chopped ham
- 2 c. shredded cheddar cheese
- 10 medium eggs
- 1 c. coconut milk
- Salt
- black pepper
- olive oil

Directions:

1. Spray a baking dish with olive oil.
2. In a bowl, mix onion with ham, cheese, eggs, coconut milk, salt and pepper and stir well.
3. Pour this into the baking dish and spread evenly.
4. Add the water to your instant pot, add the steamer basket, add the baking dish inside, cover and cook on Manual for 25 minutes.
5. Slice, divide between plates and serve for breakfast.
6. Enjoy!

Nutrition information: 192 Calories, 6g Carbs, 8g Protein, 4g Fat

Chocolate Oatmeal

Servings: 4

Ingredients

- 1 c. coconut milk
- 2½ tbsps. cocoa powder
- 4 c. water
- 2 c. shredded coconut
- 1 tsp. vanilla extract
- 1 tsp. cinnamon powder
- 10 oz. pitted cherries

Directions:

1. In your instant pot, mix coconut milk with water, cocoa powder, coconut, vanilla extract, cinnamon and cherries, stir, cover and cook on High for 10 minutes.
2. Stir your chocolate oatmeal once again, divide into bowls and serve for breakfast.
3. Enjoy!

Nutrition information: 183 Calories, 5g Carbs, 7g Protein, 4g Fat

Almond and Chia Breakfast

Servings: 2

Ingredients

- 2 tbsps. chopped almonds
- 1 tbsp. chia seeds
- 2 tbsps. roasted pepitas
- 1/3 c. coconut milk
- 1/3 c. water
- A handful blueberries

Directions:

1. In your food processor, mix pepitas with almonds and pulse them well.
2. In your instant pot, mix chia seeds with water and coconut milk and stir.
3. Add pepitas mix, stir, cover pot and cook on High for 5 minutes.
4. Add strawberries, toss a bit, divide into 2 bowls and serve for breakfast.
5. Enjoy!

Nutrition information: 150 Calories, 4g Carbs, 2g Protein, 1g Fat

Strawberries and Coconut Breakfast

Servings: 2

Ingredients

- 3 tbsps. coconut flakes
- 2 tbsps. chopped strawberries
- 1 c. water
- 2/3 c. coconut milk
- ½ tsp. stevia

Directions:

1. In your instant pot, mix strawberries with coconut flakes, water, milk and stevia, stir, cover and cook on High for 10 minutes.
2. Divide into 2 bowls and serve for breakfast.
3. Enjoy!

Nutritional information: 110 Calories, 3g Carbs, 3g Protein, 5g Fat

Vegetables

Mashed Cauliflower

Servings: 4

Ingredients:

- 1 Cauliflower Head
- 3 tbsps. Melted butter
- 1 c. Water
- ¼ tsp. Pepper
- ½ tsp. Salt

Directions:

1. Chop the cauliflower and place inside the steamer basket.
2. Pour the water into the Instant Pot and lower the basket.
3. Close the lid, set it to MANUAL, and cook on HIGH for 4 minutes.
4. Do a quick pressure release.
5. Mash the cauliflower with a potato masher or in a food processor, and stir in the remaining ingredients.
6. Serve and enjoy!

Nutritional Info: 113 Calories, 5.9g Fat, 4.1g carbs, 3g protein

Buttered Asparagus

Servings: 4

Ingredients:

- 1 lb. Trimmed asparagus
- 3 Garlic cloves
- 3 tbsps. Softened butter
- 3 tbsps. Grated Parmesan cheese

Directions:

1. In the center of a foil piece, place the asparagus and garlic and top with butter.
2. Curve the edges of foil slightly to avoid the leakage of butter.
3. In the bottom of Instant Pot, arrange a steamer basket and pour 1 cup of water.
4. Place the asparagus on the steamer basket.
5. Close the lid, select STEAM, and cook for 8 minutes.
6. Press CANCEL and do a quick pressure release.
7. Remove the lid and transfer the asparagus onto serving plates.
8. Sprinkle with Parmesan and serve.

Nutritional Info:108 Calories, 9.1g Fat, 2.8g Carbs, 3.2g Protein

Ketogenic Eggplants and Spinach

Servings: 4

Ingredients:

- 2 tbsps. Coconut oil
- 4 c. Cubed eggplants
- 2 c. Chopped spinach
- 1 tsp. Five spice powder
- 1 c. Vegetable broth
- ½ c. Coconut milk
- 1 tsp. Chili powder
- 1 tsp. Salt
- ½ tsp. Pepper

Directions:

1. Set the Instant Pot to SAUTÉ and melt the coconut oil in it.
2. Add the eggplant cubes and cook for about 2 minutes.
3. Stir in the spinach and the seasonings.
4. Add the vegetable broth and coconut milk and stir to combine.
5. Close the lid and press MANUAL. Cook on HIGH for 4 minutes.
6. Release the pressure quickly.
7. Serve and enjoy!

Nutritional Info: 164 Calories, 14.1g Fat, 3.6g Carbs, 3.2g Protein

Tomato with Tofu

Servings: 4

Ingredients:

- 1 c. Diced tomatoes
- 1 Cubed block firm tofu
- ½ c. Vegetable broth
- 2 tsps. Italian seasoning
- 2 tbsps. Jarred banana pepper rings
- 1 tbsp. Olive oil

Directions:

1. Place all of the ingredients in the Instant Pot. Stir to combine the mixture well.
2. Close the lid and hit MANUAL. Cook for 4 minutes on HIGH.
3. Do a quick pressure release.
4. Serve and enjoy!

Nutritional Info:68 Calories, 5.4g Fat, 2.3g Carbs, 2.9g Protein

Dijon and Lemon Artichokes

Servings: 4

Ingredients:

- 1½ c. Water
- 2 Artichokes
- 1 Lemon
- ¼ tsp. Salt
- ¼ tsp. Pepper
- 2 tbsps. Dijon mustard
- 2 tbsps. Olive oil
- 1 Lemon wedge

Directions:

1. Wash the artichokes well and trim them. Rub them with the lemon wedge.
2. Pour the water into the Instant Pot and lower the steamer basket.
3. Place the artichokes in the basket.
4. Close the lid and cook for 20 minutes on HIGH.
5. Do a natural pressure release, about 10 minutes. Quick release the remaining pressure.
6. In a small bowl, mix together the lemon juice, mustard, olive oil, salt, and pepper.
7. Serve artichokes with the sauce.
8. Enjoy!

Nutritional Info: 108 Calories, 7.5g Fat, 5.4g Carbs, 3.1g Protein

Zesty Broccoli and Cauliflower Bowl

Servings: 4

Ingredients:

- 1 Chopped cauliflower head
- 1 lb. Broccoli florets
- 1 tbsp. Capers
- 1 Grapefruit
- ¼ tsp. Pepper
- 4 tbsps. Olive oil
- ½ tsp. Salt
- 1½ c. Water

Directions:

1. Pour the water into the Instant Pot and lower the steamer basket.
2. Place the cauliflower and broccoli inside the steamer basket.
3. Close the lid and Cook on STEAM for 6 minutes.
4. Meanwhile, place the juice, zest, salt, pepper, capers, and oil in a bowl. Whisk to combine.
5. Do a quick pressure release and transfer the veggies to a bowl.
6. Pour the dressing over. Enjoy!

Nutritional Info:195 Calories, 14.5g Fat, 11g Carbs, 4.8g Protein

Cauliflower Patties

Servings: 6

Ingredients:

- 1 Chopped cauliflower head
- 1 c. Shredded Cheddar cheese
- 2 Eggs
- ¼ c. Grated Parmesan cheese
- 1 c. Ground almonds
- 3 tbsps. Olive oil
- 1 tsp. Italian seasoning
- ½ tsp. Salt
- ¼ tsp. Pepper
- ¼ tsp. Garlic powder
- 3 c. Water

Directions:

1. Pour half of the water into the Instant Pot.
2. Place the cauliflower in the steamer basket and lower it into the pot.
3. Close the lid and cook on HIGH for 5 minutes.
4. Do a quick pressure release and let the cauliflower cool until safe to handle.
5. Transfer the cauliflower to a food processor. Pulse until finely ground.
6. Transfer the ground cauliflower to a bowl along with the eggs, parmesan, almonds, Italian seasoning, salt, pepper, garlic powder, and ¾ of the cheddar. Mix with your hands until fully incorporated.
7. Make patties out of the mixture.
8. Discard the water from the pot and wipe it clean.
9. Set the Instant Pot to SAUTÉ. Heat half of the oil in the pot and add half of the patties. Cook until golden on all sides. Repeat with the other half. Press CANCEL.
10. Transfer the patties to a greased baking dish. Top with the remaining cheese.
11. Pour the remaining water into the pot and lower the dish.
12. Close the lid and cook for 2 minutes on HIGH.
13. Release the pressure quickly.
14. Serve and enjoy!

Nutritional Info: 278 Calories, 23.9g Fat, 3.4g Carbs, 12.3g Protein

Southern Collard Greens

Servings: 5

Ingredients:

- 2 bunches Collard greens
- 2 tbsps. Olive oil
- 1 Yellow onion
- 3 Minced garlic cloves
- Red pepper flakes
- 1 c. Water
- Salt

Directions:

1. Remove the tough stems of collard greens and then, cut into thin strands.
2. Place olive oil in the Instant Pot and select "Sauté". Then add the onion and cook for about 4-5 minutes.
3. Add the garlic and red pepper flakes and cook for about 1 minute.
4. Select the "Cancel" and stir in collard greens and water.
5. While the lid is secured, set pressure valve to "Seal" position.
6. Select "Manual" and cook for 3 minutes under "High Pressure".
7. Select the "Cancel" and carefully do a Quick release.
8. Remove the lid and stir in salt.
9. Serve hot.

Nutritional Info:106 Calories, 6.9g Fat, 2.38g Carbs, 4.3g Protein

Nicely Flavored Swiss Chard

Servings: 6

Ingredients:

- 2 Swiss chard
- 2 tbsps. Olive oil
- ¼ tsp. Ground cumin
- 1/8 tsp. Crushed red pepper flakes
- 1/8 tsp. Cayenne pepper
- 1/3 c. Water

Directions:

1. In the pot of Instant Pot, add all ingredients and stir to combine.
2. Secure the lid and place the pressure valve to "Seal" position.
3. Select "Manual" and cook under "High Pressure" for about 3 minutes.
4. Select the "Cancel" and carefully do a Natural release.
5. Remove the lid and serve.

Nutritional Info:50 Calories, 4.8g Fat, 0.31g Carbs, 0.9g Protein

American Style Kale

Servings: 4

Ingredients:

- 1 tbsp. Olive oil
- 3 Garlic cloves
- 1 lb. Chopped fresh kale
- ½ c. Water
- Salt
- Black pepper
- 1 tbsp. Lemon juice

Directions:

1. Place the oil in the Instant Pot and select "Sauté". Then add the garlic and cook for about 1 minute.
2. Add the kale and cook for about 1-2 minutes.
3. Select the "Cancel" and stir in water, salt and black pepper.
4. While the lid is secured, set the pressure valve to "Seal" position.
5. Select "Manual" and cook under "High Pressure" for about 5 minutes.
6. Select "Cancel" option and do a Quick release.
7. Open the lid and stir in lemon juice.
8. Serve hot.

Nutritional Info:90 Calories, 12.7g Fat, 3.17g Carbs, 3.6g Protein

Meat and seafood

Sockeye Salmon

Servings: 4

Ingredients:

- 4 Sockeye salmon fillets
- 1 tsp. Dijon mustard
- ¼ tsp. Minced garlic
- 1 tbsp. Lemon juice
- ¼ tsp. Onion powder
- ¼ tsp. Lemon pepper
- ½ tsp. Garlic powder
- ¼ tsp. Salt
- 2 tbsps. Olive oil
- 1½ c. Water

Directions:

1. In a bowl, combine the mustard, garlic, lemon juice, onion powder, lemon pepper, garlic powder, salt, and olive oil. Brush the spice mixture over the salmon fillets.
2. Pour the water into the Instant Pot. Lower the trivet.
3. Place the salmon fillets on the rack and close the lid.
4. Set the Instant Pot to MANUAL and cook at low pressure for 7 minutes.
5. Release the pressure quickly.
6. Serve and enjoy!

Nutritional Info:

353 Calories, 25g Fat, 0.6g Carbs, 40.6g Protein

Shrimp Zoodles

Servings: 4

Ingredients:

- 4 c. Zoodles
- 1 tbsp. Chopped basil
- 2 tbsps. Ghee
- 1 lb. Shrimp
- 1 c. Vegetable stock
- 2 Minced garlic cloves
- 2 tbsps. Olive oil
- ½ Lemon
- ½ tsp. Paprika

Directions:

1. Set your Instant Pot to SAUTÉ and melt the ghee with the olive oil in it.
2. Add garlic and cook for 1 minute.
3. Add the lemon juice and shrimp and cook for another minute.
4. Stir in the remaining ingredients and close the lid.
5. Set the Instant Pot to MANUAL and cook at low pressure for 5 minutes.
6. Do a quick pressure release.
7. Serve and enjoy!

Nutritional Info: 277 Calories, 15.6g Fat, 5.9g Carbs, 27.5g Protein

Cherry Tomato Mackerel

Servings: 4

Ingredients:

- 4 Mackerel fillets
- ¼ tsp. Onion powder
- ¼ tsp. Lemon pepper
- ¼ tsp. Garlic powder
- ¼ tsp. Salt
- 2 c. Cherry tomatoes
- 3 tbsps. Melted butter
- 1½ c. Water
- 1 tbsp. black olives

Directions:

1. Grease a baking dish that fits inside the Instant Pot, with some cooking spray.
2. Arrange the cherry tomatoes at the bottom of the dish. Top with the mackerel fillets and sprinkle with all of the spices. Drizzle the melted butter over.
3. Pour water into Instant Pot and lower the trivet.
4. Place the baking dish on the trivet. Close the lid.
5. Set the Instant Pot to MANUAL and cook at low pressure for 7 minutes.
6. Do a quick pressure release.
7. Serve and enjoy!

Nutritional Info: 325 Calories, 24.5g Fat, 2.7g Carbs, 21.9g Protein

Lobster Pasta

Servings: 4

Ingredients:

- 3 Lobster tails
- 1 c. Half & half
- 2c. Water
- 4 c. Zoodles
- 1 tbsp. Arrowroot
- 1 tbsp. Melted butter
- 1 c. Shredded Gruyere cheese
- 1 tbsp. Worcestershire sauce
- ½ tbsp. Chopped tarragon

Directions:

1. Combine the water and lobster tails in your Instant Pot.
2. Close the lid and cook for 5 minutes on low pressure.
3. Do a quick pressure release and transfer the lobster to a plate. Let it cool until easy to handle. Spoon out the meat from the tails and place in a bowl.
4. Discard the cooking liquid from the pot and combine the Half & Half, arrowroot, butter, and Worcestershire sauce in it.
5. Set the Instant Pot to SAUTÉ and cook the sauce for 2 minutes.
6. Stir in the lobster, zoodles, and cheese.
7. Cook for 3 minutes.
8. Sprinkle with tarragon and serve.

Nutritional Info:276 Calories, 19.5g Fat, 5.2g Carbs, 21.3g Protein

Lemon and Garlic Prawns

Servings: 4

Ingredients:

- 2 tbsps. Olive oil
- 1 lb. Prawns
- 2 tbsps. Minced garlic
- 2/3 c. Fish stock
- 1 tbsp. Butter
- 2 tbsps. Lemon juice
- 1 tbsp. Lemon zest
- Salt
- Pepper

Directions:

1. Melt the butter with the oil in your Instant Pot on SAUTÉ.
2. Stir in the remaining ingredients.
3. Close the lid and select MANUAL option on the Instant Pot. Cook the prawns at low pressure for 5 minutes.
4. Do a quick pressure release and serve.

Nutritional Info:236 Calories, 12.2g Fat, 3.4g Carbs, 27.1g Protein

Tender Beef Pot Roast

Servings: 6

Ingredients:

- 1 Sliced onion
- 2 tbsps. Minced garlic
- 2½ lbs. Beef roast
- 2 tbsps. Sugar-free steak sauce
- 2 Chopped celery stalks
- 1 Chopped bell pepper
- 2 tbsps. Olive oil
- 1 c. Beef broth
- 1 tbsp. Balsamic vinegar
- 1½ tbsps. Italian seasoning

Directions:

1. Heat 1 tbsp. of olive oil in the Instant Pot on SAUTÉ.
2. Add the beef and sear it on all sides until browned, about 5 minutes in total. Transfer to a plate.
3. Heat the remaining oil in the Instant Pot and add the onions, celery, and pepper. Cook for a few minutes, until soft.
4. Add garlic and cook for 30 seconds.
5. Return the meat to the pot.
6. In a bowl, whisk together the vinegar, broth, and Italian Seasoning. Pour the mixture over the beef.
7. Close the lid and cook on HIGH for 40 minutes.
8. Release the pressure naturally.
9. Serve and enjoy!

Nutritional Info: 603 Calories, 40.4g Fat, 4.5g Carbs, 51.7g Protein

Knorr Demi-Glace Brisket

Servings: 4

Ingredients:

- 2 tbsps. Olive oil
- 2 lbs. Beef brisket
- 1 Chopped onion
- 2 Chopped celery stalks
- 2 Minced garlic cloves
- 2 Bay leaves
- 1¼ c. Beef broth
- 2 tbsps. Knorr Demi-glace sauce
- 1 tbsp. Worcestershire sauce
- ½ tsp. Salt
- ½ tsp. Black pepper

Directions:

1. Season the brisket with salt and pepper.
2. Heat a tablespoon of olive oil in your Instant Pot on SAUTÉ and add the beef. Sear for about 2 minutes per side. Transfer to a plate.
3. Heat the other tablespoon of oil and add the onions and celery. Cook until soft. Stir in the garlic and cook for another minute.
4. Return beef to your pot and add the bay leaves.
5. In a bowl, whisk together the broth and sauces and pour the mixture over the beef.
6. Close the lid and cook on MEAT/STEW for 1 hour.
7. Do a natural pressure release.
8. Serve and enjoy!

*Nutritional Info:*735 Calories, 58.3g Fat, 6.1g Carbs, 45.8g Protein

Balsamic-Glazed Pork Loin

Servings: 4

Ingredients:

- 1 Minced garlic clove
- 1 tsp. Sage
- 2 lbs. Pork loin
- ½ c. Beef broth
- ½ tsp. Pepper
  Glaze:
- 1 tbsp. Arrowroot
- ¼ c. Balsamic vinegar
- ½ c. Swerve
- 2 tbsps. Coconut aminos
- ½ c. Water

Directions:

1. Rub the pork with the sage, pepper, and garlic. Place it inside the Instant Pot and pour the broth over.
2. Close lid tightly and set the IP to MANUAL. Cook on HIGH for 1 hour.
3. Release the pressure naturally for 10 minutes. Quick release the remaining pressure.
4. Meanwhile, whisk together the glaze ingredients.
5. You can either brush the mixture over the pork loin and sear on SAUTÉ for a few minutes, or shred the meat, pour the sauce over and cook on SAUTÉ for 2-3 minutes.
6. Serve and enjoy!

Nutritional Info: 568 Calories, 31.8g Fat, 12.5g Carbs, 42.8g Protein

French Onion Pork Chops

Servings: 4

Ingredients:

- 4 Pork chops
- 10 oz. French onion soup
- ½ c. Sour cream
- 10 oz. Chicken broth

Directions:

1. Place pork chops in the IP and pour the broth over.
2. Close the lid and cook on HIGH for 12 minutes.
3. Release the pressure naturally.
4. Whisk together the sour cream and French onion soup and pour the mixture over the pork.
5. Set the Instant Pot to SAUTÉ and cook for about 6–8 minutes.
6. Serve and enjoy!

Nutritional Info:

365 Calories, 26.9g Fat, 6.9g Carbs, 21.5g Protein

Herb Meatloaf

Servings: 6

Ingredients:

- 3 tbsps. Olive oil
- 1 tsp. Oregano
- 2 tsps. Thyme
- 1 tsp. Rosemary
- ½ tsp. Parsley
- 2 lbs. Ground beef
- ¼ tsp. Pepper
- 2 Eggs
- 3 tbsps. Almond flour
- 1 tsp. Garlic salt
- 1½ c. Water

Directions:

1. Pour the water into your Instant Pot and lower the trivet.
2. Grease a loaf pan that fits inside your Instant Pot with the olive oil.
3. Place the remaining ingredients in a large bowl. Mix with your hands until well incorporated. Transfer the mixture to the loaf pan and press firmly.
4. Place the loaf pan on the trivet and close the lid.
5. Set the Instant Pot to MANUAL and cook on HIGH for 30 minutes.
6. Release pressure naturally for 10 minutes. Quick release the remaining pressure.
7. Serve and enjoy!

Nutritional Info:531 Calories, 46.3g Fat, 0.7g Carbs, 26.2g Protein

Soup & Stews

Pomodoro Soup with Basil

Servings: 4

Ingredients:

- 2 tbsps. Olive oil
- ½ Diced onion
- 2 tbsps. Tomato paste
- 3 c. Vegetable broth
- 28 oz. Diced tomatoes
- Chopped basil
- 1 tsp. Balsamic vinegar
- ½ c. Shredded Cheddar cheese

Directions:

1. Set your Instant Pot on SAUTÉ and heat the oil in it. Add the onions and sauté for 3–4 minutes.
2. Stir in the tomato paste and cook for 30–60 seconds.
3. Pour the broth over and stir in the tomatoes.
4. Close the lid and cook on SOUP for 10 minutes.
5. Release the pressure naturally.
6. Stir in half of the basil and the balsamic vinegar. Use a hand blender to blend the mixture until smooth.
7. Top with the remaining basil and serve. Enjoy!

Nutritional Info:196 Calories, 13.2g Fat, 8.8g Carbs, 9.4g Protein

Fish Stew

Servings: 6

Ingredients:

- 3 c. Fish stock
- 1 Diced onion
- 1 c. Chopped broccoli
- 2 c. Chopped celery stalks
- 1½ c. Diced cauliflower
- 1 Sliced carrot
- 1 lb. Chopped white fish fillets
- 1 c. Heavy cream
- 1 Bay leaf
- 2 tbsps. Butter
- ¼ tsp. Pepper
- ½ tsp. Salt
- ¼ tsp. Garlic powder

Directions:

1. Set your Instant Pot to SAUTÉ and melt the butter in it. Add onion and carrots (if using), and cook for 3 minutes.
2. Stir in the remaining ingredients.
3. Close the lid and hit MANUAL. Cook for 4 minutes on HIGH.
4. Do a natural pressure release. Discard the bay leaf.
5. Serve and enjoy!

Nutritional Info:

294 Calories, 18g Fat, 6.1g Carbs, 24.2g Protein

Bolognese Soup

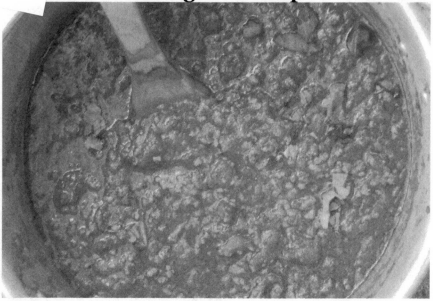

Servings: 4

Ingredients:

- 1 lb. Ground beef
- 1 c. Chopped onion
- ½ tsp. Oregano
- ½ tsp. Thyme
- ¼ tsp. Tomato puree
- 14 oz. Diced tomatoes
- 2 tsps. Minced garlic
- 2 c. Diced cauliflower
- 3 c. Chicken broth
- ½ tsp. Pepper
- ½ tsp. Salt
- 4 tbsps. Olive oil
- 1 tbsp. Chopped basil

Directions:

1. Set the Instant Pot to SAUTÉ and heat the olive oil in it. Add the onions and cook for about 3 minutes.
2. Stir in the garlic and cook for 1 more minute.
3. Add the beef and cook until browned.
4. Stir in the tomatoes and tomato puree. Cook for about 2 minutes.
5. Add the broth, salt, and pepper, and stir to combine, and close the lid.
6. Cook at high pressure for 5 minutes.
7. Do a quick pressure release and stir in the cauliflower.
8. Cook at high pressure for another 5 minutes.
9. Let the pressure drop naturally.
10. Serve topped with chopped basil.
11. Enjoy!

Nutritional Info:411 Calories, 22.5g Fat, 8.5g Carbs, 40.7g Protein

Keto Chili

Servings: 4

Ingredients:

- 2 tbsps. Olive oil
- ½ tsp. Cumin
- 2 tbsps. Tomato paste
- 2 lbs. Ground beef
- 1 c. Diced tomatoes
- 1 tsp. Chili powder
- 1 Diced onion
- 1 c. Beef broth
- 1 tsp. Minced garlic
- Salt
- Pepper

Directions:

1. Set the Instant Pot to SAUTÉ and heat the olive oil in it.
2. Cook the onions for about 2 minutes. Add garlic and cook for 1 minute.
3. Add the beef and cook until it is browned, breaking it with a spatula.
4. Stir in the tomato paste and spices and cook for 1 more minute.
5. Stir in the broth and tomatoes.
6. Close the lid and cook for 30 minutes on MEAT/STEW.
7. Do a quick pressure release.
8. Serve and enjoy!

Nutritional Info:505 Calories, 33.5g Fat, 5.1g Carbs, 42.7g Protein

Mexican Chicken Soup

Servings: 8

Ingredients:

- 2 c. Shredded chicken
- 4 tbsps. Olive oil
- ½ c. Chopped cilantro
- 8 c. Chicken broth
- 1/3 c. Salsa
- 1 tsp. Onion powder
- ½ c. Chopped scallions
- 4 oz. Chopped green chilies
- ½ tsp. Minced habanero
- 1 c. Chopped celery root
- 1 tsp. Cumin
- 1 tsp. Garlic powder
- Salt
- Pepper

Directions:

1. Place everything in the Instant Pot. Give it a good stir to combine.
2. Close the lid and set Instant Pot to SOUP. Cook for 10 minutes.
3. When cooking is complete, use a natural pressure release.
4. Serve and enjoy!

Nutritional Info:204 Calories, 14g Fat, 4.2g Carbs, 14.4g Protein

Creamy Broccoli and Cheese Soup

Servings: 6

Ingredients:

- 3 c. Vegetable broth
- 3 tbsps. Butter
- 4 American cheese slices
- 1 c. Shredded Pepper Jack cheese
- 2 tbsps. Almond flour
- ½ c. Grated Parmesan cheese
- 5 c. Broccoli florets
- 1 tsp. Minced Garlic
- 1 c. Half & half
- ½ Diced onion
- 1 tsp. Dill
- ¼ tsp. Turmeric

Directions:

1. Melt the butter in your Instant Pot on SAUTÉ. Add the onions and cook until they become soft.
2. Add garlic and cook for one minute.
3. Stir in the broccoli and broth and close the lid.
4. Set the Instant Pot to MANUAL and cook on HIGH for 5 minutes.
5. Do a quick pressure release.
6. Stir in the remaining ingredients and close the lid again.
7. Cook at high pressure for 1 more minute.
8. Release the pressure quickly.
9. Blend the soup with a hand blender until smooth.
10. Serve and enjoy!

Nutritional Info: 250 Calories, 18.5g Fat, 7.8g Carbs, 12.7g Protein

Pressure-Cooked Beef Stew

Servings: 4

Ingredients:

- 3 tbsps. Olive oil
- 1 lb. Cubed beef
- 3 c. Beef broth
- ½ Diced onion
- 28 oz. Diced tomatoes
- 2 tbsps. Minced garlic
- 1 Sliced carrot
- 1 Chopped red bell pepper
- 2 tbsps. Chopped parsley
- 1 tsp. Thyme
- 1 Bay leaf

Directions:

1. Set your Instant Pot to SAUTÉ and heat the olive oil in it.
2. Add onions and cook until softened.
3. Add the thyme and garlic and cook until they become fragrant, about one minute.
4. Add the beef and cook it until browned on all sides.
5. Dump the rest of the ingredients into the Instant Pot and stir to combine.
6. While lid is closed, set the Instant Pot to MANUAL. Cook on HIGH for 20 minutes.
7. When cooking is complete, wait for five minutes before releasing the pressure quickly.
8. Serve and enjoy!

Nutritional Info:382 Calories, 25g Fat, 10.6g Carbs, 26.3g Protein

Great Cauliflower Soup

Servings: 5

Ingredients:

- 1 Chopped yellow onion
- 1 c. Coconut milk
- 1 Cauliflower head
- 1 c. Shredded cheddar cheese
- 3 c. Chicken stock
- Salt
- Black pepper
- 1 tsp. Garlic powder
- 2 tbsps. Olive oil
- 4 oz. Cubed cream cheese

Directions:

1. First of all, please make sure you've all the ingredients available. Set your instant pot on sauté mode, add oil, heat it up, add onion, stir and cook properly for about 2 to 5 minutes.
2. Then add cauliflower, stir and cook properly for about 2 minutes more.
3. Add stock, mil and garlic powder, stir, cover & cook properly on High for about 5 to 10 minutes.
4. One thing remains to be done. Now add cream cheese & pulse everything using an immersion blender.
5. Finally add cheddar cheese, stir soup, ladle into bowls & serve.

Nutritional Info:261 Calories, 4g Fat, 7g Carbs, 8g Protein

Chili Tomato Pork Stew

Servings: 4

Ingredients:

- 1 lb. Pork shoulder
- 1 Diced red onion
- 2 Minced garlic cloves
- 2 tbsps. Coconut oil
- 6 oz. Sliced mushrooms
- 1 Chopped green bell pepper
- 1 Chopped red bell pepper
- 4 c. Beef broth
- 1 tbsp. Lime juice
- ½ c. Tomato paste
- 2 tsps. Chili powder
- 2 tsps. Ground cumin
- 1 tbsp. Chopped cilantro
- 1 tsp. Smoked paprika
- 1 tsp. Salt
- 1 tsp. black pepper

Directions:

1. Rinse the pork shoulder, pat dry. Cut into chunks.
2. Press Sauté button on Instant Pot. Heat the coconut oil.
3. Add onion, garlic. Sweat for 1 minute. Add pork shoulder. Brown on all sides.
4. Add mushrooms, bell peppers. Sauté until vegetables have softened.
5. Press Keep Warm/Cancel button to stop Sauté mode.
6. Add rest of ingredients. Stir well.
7. Close and seal lid. Press Soup button. Cook for 30 minutes.
8. When timer beeps, quick-release or naturally release pressure. Open lid carefully. Stir ingredients.
9. Serve.

Nutritional Info: 350 Calories, 28g Fat, 10g Carbs, 20g Protein

Rich Turkey Stew

Servings: 5

Ingredients:

- 1 Chopped yellow onion
- 1½ tbsps. Cranberry sauce
- 1 tsp. Minced garlic
- 3 Chopped celery stalks
- 5 c. Turkey stock
- 2 Chopped carrots
- Salt
- 15 oz. Chopped tomatoes
- Black pepper
- 3 c. Shredded turkey meat
- 1½ tbsps. Avocado oil

Directions:

1. First of all, please make sure you've all the ingredients available. Then set your instant pot on Sauté mode, add oil, heat it up, add carrots, celery & onions, stir and cook properly for about 2 to 5 minutes.
2. One thing remains to be done. Now add tomatoes, stock, cranberry sauce, garlic, meat, salt and pepper, stir, cover, cook properly on Low for about 30 to 35 minutes, divide into bowls and serve.
3. Finally enjoy!

Nutritional Info: 200 Calories, 4g Fat, 6g Carbs, 16g Protein

Instant Celeriac and Leek Soup

Servings: 6

Ingredients:

- 2 tbsps. butter
- 2 sliced leeks
- 1 tsp. kosher salt
- 3 crushed cloves garlic
- 3 sprigs thyme, fresh
- 1 tsp. oregano, dry
- 2 leaves bay
- ¾ c. white wine
- 4 c. water
- 4 chopped celeriac root
- 1 c. heavy cream

Directions:

1. Melt butter in the Instant Pot. Add leeks and garlic cloves and press saute to soften them.
2. Kill the heat and set aside.
3. Add in the bay leaves, celeriac root, thyme, white wine, oregano, and water as you stir.
4. Select Manual high pressure and wait for 10 minutes.
5. Open the pot as you select Quick release.
6. Add the cream puree the soup to obtain a desired rich creamy consistency.
7. Serve immediately.

Nutritional Info: 222.83 Calories, 18.7g Fat, 8.11g Carbs, 1.7g Protein

Instant Creamy Swiss chard Soup

Servings: 6

Ingredients:

- 1½ tbsps. butter
- 1½ lbs. Swiss chard
- 3 c. water
- ½ c. chopped onion
- 3 minced cloves garlic
- 1 tsp. Italian seasonings
- ½ c. heavy cream
- ½ c. grated cottage cheese
- Salt
- Ground black pepper

Directions:

1. Press Sauté function and melt butter in your Instant Pot. Cook the onion, add garlic and cover with water.
2. Bring to boil, add coarsely chopped Swiss chard and seasonings.
3. Close the lead, select Manual high pressure set for 10 minutes.
4. Release pressure using the Normal method - release vapor through the valve.
5. Transfer the soup to a blender and process, adding heavy cream until soup is creamy and smooth. Adjust salt and pepper to taste.
6. Serve warm with grated cheese.

Nutritional Info: 139.9 Calories, 4.9g Fat, 5.3g Carbs, 4.9g Protein

Divine Cabbage Beef Soup

Servings: 6

Ingredients:

- 1 lb. lean ground beef
- 1 head chopped green cabbage
- 1 head chopped red cabbage
- 1 chopped celery stalk
- 28 oz. tomatoes, diced
- 3 c. water
- 1 tsp. salt
- 1 tsp. black pepper, ground
- 1 tbsp. chopped parsley

Directions:

1. Press Sauté button on Instant Pot.
2. Add ground beef. Sauté until no longer pink; drain.
3. Press Keep Warm/Cancel setting to stop Sauté mode.
4. Return ground beef to Instant Pot. Add cabbage, celery, diced tomatoes, water, parsley, salt, and pepper. Stir well.
5. Close and seal lid. Press Meat/Stew. Cook on High Pressure for 20 minutes.
6. Once done, Instant Pot will switch to Keep Warm mode.
7. Remain in Keep Warm mode for 10 minutes.
8. When done, use Quick-Release. Open lid carefully. Stir ingredients.
9. Serve. Garnish with fresh parsley.

Nutritional Info: 115 Calories, 4.4g Fat, 11g Carbs, 11g Protein

Creamy Delicious Broccoli Soup

Servings: 4

Ingredients:

- 1 head chopped broccoli
- 4 minced garlic cloves
- 3 c. vegetable broth
- 1 c. heavy cream
- 3 c. shredded cheddar cheese
- 1 tsp. salt
- 1 tsp. black pepper, ground

Directions:

1. In your Instant Pot, add broccoli florets, garlic, vegetable stock, heavy cream, and shredded cheese. Stir well.
2. Close and seal lid. Press Soup button. Cook for 30 minutes.
3. When done, naturally release or quick-release pressure. Open lid carefully. Stir.
4. Serve.

Nutritional Info: 250 Calories, 25g Fat, 5g Carbs, 14g Protein

Delicious Broccoli and Bacon Soup

Servings: 4

Ingredients:

- 4 slices bacon, smoked
- 1 tsp. olive oil
- 2 chopped heads broccoli
- 1 chopped leek
- 1 chopped stalk celery
- 1 c. spinach, frozen
- Parmesan cheese
- 4 c. water
- Salt
- Black pepper

Directions:

1. Set your Instant Pot to Sauté and add the oil.
2. Cook the bacon slice until the bacon is crisp.
3. When cooked, remove the bacon to a plate and set aside
4. Add all the vegetables from the list and then stir very well to combine everything.
5. Cover with water and tuck the Parmesan rind in.
6. Cancel Sauté mode, set to Manual for 5 minutes on high pressure.
7. Remove lid, retrieve the rind of the Parmesan, scraping any melted cheese into the pot then use a stick blender to purée your soup.
8. Add pepper and salt for seaasoning.
9. Serve hot ladled into bowls.

Nutritional Info: 222.1 Calories, 18.89g Fat, 7g Carbs, 7.4g Protein

Side Dishes

Napa Cabbage Side Salad

Servings: 6

Ingredients:

- Salt
- Ground black pepper
- 1 lb. chopped napa cabbage
- 1 carrot, julienned
- 2 tbsps. veggie stock
- ½ c. daikon radish
- 3 minced garlic cloves
- 3 chopped green onion stalks
- 1 tbsp. coconut aminos
- 3 tbsps. chili flakes
- 1 tbsp. olive oil
- ½ inch grated ginger

Directions:

1. In a bowl, mix black pepper, cabbage and salt, massage well for 10 minutes, cover and leave aside for 30 minutes.
2. In another bowl, mix chili flakes with aminos, garlic, oil and ginger and stir whisk well.
3. Drain cabbage well, transfer to your instant pot, add stock, carrots, green onions, radish and the chili paste you made, stir, cover and cook on High for 5 minutes.
4. Place on plates and serve!

Nutritional Info:100 Calories, 3g Fat, 5g Carbs, 2g Protein

Asian Brussels Sprouts

Servings: 4

Ingredients:

- 1 lb. halved Brussels sprouts
- 3 tbsps. chicken stock
- Salt
- Black pepper
- 1 tsp. toasted sesame seeds
- 1 tbsp. chopped green onions
- 1½ tbsps. stevia
- 1 tbsp. coconut aminos
- 2 tbsp. olive oil
- 1 tbsp. keto sriracha sauce
-

Directions:

1. In a bowl, mix oil with coconut aminos, sriracha, stevia, salt and black pepper and whisk well.
2. Put Brussels sprouts in your instant pot, add sriracha mix, stock, green onions and sesame seeds, stir, cover and cook on High for 4 minutes.
3. Serve and enjoy!

Nutritional Info:110 Calories, 4 g Fat, 4g Carbs, 2g Protein

Cauliflower and Parmesan

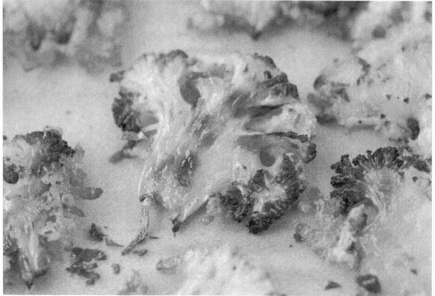

Servings: 6

Ingredients:

- 1 cauliflower head
- ½ c. veggie stock
- 2 minced garlic cloves
- Salt
- Black pepper
- 1/3 c. grated parmesan
- 1 tbsp. chopped parsley
- 3 tbsps. olive oil

Directions:

1. In a bowl, mix oil with garlic, salt, pepper and cauliflower florets, toss and transfer to your instant pot.
2. Add stock, cover pot and cook on High for 4 minutes.
3. Add parsley and parmesan, toss, divide between plates and serve as a side dish.
4. Enjoy!

Nutritional Info: 120 Calories, 2g Fat, 5g Carbs, 3g Protein

Swiss Chard and Garlic

Servings: 2

Ingredients:

- 2 tbsps. ghee
- 3 tbsps. lemon juice
- ½ c. chicken stock
- 4 chopped bacon slices
- 1 bunch chopped Swiss chard
- ½ tsp. garlic paste
- Salt
- Black pepper

Directions:

1. Set your instant pot on sauté mode, add bacon, stir and cook for a couple of minutes.
2. Add ghee, lemon juice and garlic paste and stir.
3. Add Swiss chard, salt, pepper and stock, cover pot and cook on High for 3 minutes.
4. Serve and enjoy!

Nutritional Info:160 Calories, 7g Fat, 6g Carbs, 4g Protein

Red Chard and Olives

Servings: 4

Ingredients:

- 2 tbsps. olive oil
- 1 bunch chopped red chard
- 3 tbsps. veggie stock
- 2 tbsps. capers
- 1 chopped yellow onion
- Juice of 1 lemon
- Salt
- Black pepper
- 1 tsp. stevia
- ¼ c. chopped Kalamata olives

Directions:

1. Set your instant pot on sauté mode, add oil, heat it up, add onion, stir and cook for 2 minutes.
2. Add stevia, olives, chard, salt, pepper and stock, stir, cover and cook on High for 3 minutes.
3. Add capers and lemon juice, stir, divide between plates and serve as a side dish.
4. Enjoy!

Nutritional Info:

123 Calories, 4g Fat, 4g Carbs, 5g Protein

Kale and Almonds

Servings: 4

Ingredients:

- 1 c. water
- 1 big kale bunch, chopped
- 1 tbsp. balsamic vinegar
- 1/3 c. toasted almonds
- 3 minced garlic cloves
- 1 small chopped yellow onion
- 2 tbsps. olive oil

Directions:

1. Set your instant pot on sauté mode, add oil, heat it up, add onion, stir and cook for 3 minutes.
2. Add garlic, water and kale, stir, cover and cook on High for 4 minutes.
3. Add salt, pepper, vinegar and almonds, toss well, divide between plates and serve as a side dish.
4. Enjoy!

Nutritional Info: 140 Calories, 6g Fat, 5g Carbs, 3g Protein

Green Cabbage and Paprika

Servings: 4

Ingredients:

- 1½ lbs. shredded green cabbage
- Salt
- Black pepper
- 3 tbsps. ghee
- 1 c. veggie stock
- ¼ tsp. sweet paprika

Directions:

1. Set your instant pot on sauté mode, add ghee, melt it, add cabbage, salt, pepper and stock, stir, cover and cook on High for 7 minutes.
2. Add paprika, toss a bit, divide between plates and serve as a side dish.
3. Enjoy!

Nutritional Info: 170 Calories, 4g Fat, 5g Carbs, 5g Protein

Cauliflower and Eggs Salad

Servings: 10

Ingredients:

- 21 oz. cauliflower, separate the florets
- 1 c. chopped red onion
- 1 c. chopped celery
- ½ c. water
- Salt
- Black pepper
- 2 tbsps. balsamic vinegar
- 1 tsp. stevia
- 4 boiled and chopped eggs
- 1 c. mayonnaise

Directions:

1. Put the water in your instant pot, add steamer basket, add cauliflower, cover pot and cook on High for 5 minutes.
2. Transfer cauliflower to a bowl, add eggs, celery and onion and toss.
3. In a separate bowl, mix mayo with salt, pepper, vinegar and stevia and whisk well.
4. Add this to your salad, toss, divide between plates and serve as a side dish.
5. Enjoy!

Nutritional Info:

171 Calories, 6g Fat, 6g Carbs, 3g Protein

Sprouts and Apple Side Dish

Servings: 4

Ingredients:

- 1 julienned green apple
- 1½ tsps. olive oil
- 4 c. alfalfa sprouts
- Salt
- Black pepper
- ¼ c. coconut milk

Directions:

1. Set your instant pot on sauté mode, add oil, heat it up, add apple and sprouts, stir, cover pot and cook on High for 5 minutes.
2. Add salt, pepper and coconut milk, stir, cover pot again and cook on High for 2 minutes more.
3. Serve and enjjoy as a side dish.
4. Enjoy!

Nutritional Info:120 Calories, 3g Fat, 3g Carbs, 3g Protein

Radishes and Chives

Servings: 2

Ingredients:

- 2 c. quartered radishes
- ½ c. chicken stock
- Salt
- Black pepper
- 2 tbsps. melted ghee
- 1 tbsp. chopped chives
- 1 tbsp. grated lemon zest

Directions:

1. In your instant pot, mix radishes with stock, salt, pepper and lemon zest, stir, cover pot and cook on High for 7 minutes.
2. Add melted ghee, toss a bit, divide between plates, sprinkle chives on top and serve as a side dish.
3. Enjoy!

Nutritional Info: 102 Calories, 4g Fat, 6g Carbs, 5g Protein

Celery and Rosemary Side Dish

Servings: 4

Ingredients:

- 1 lb. cubed celery
- 1 c. water
- 2 minced garlic cloves
- Salt
- black pepper
- ¼ tsp. dry rosemary
- 1 tbsp. olive oil

Directions:

1. Put the water in your instant pot, add steamer basket, add celery cubes inside, cover pot and cook on High for 4 minutes.
2. In a bowl, mix oil with garlic and rosemary and whisk well.
3. Add steamed celery, toss well, spread on a lined baking sheet and introduce in a preheated broiler for 3 minutes.
4. Serve and enjoy as a side dish.

Nutritional Info:100 Calories, 3g Fat, 8g Carbs, 3g Protein

Celeriac Fries

Servings: 4

Ingredients

- 2 big peeled celeriac
- 1 c. water
- Salt
- ¼ tsp. baking soda
- Olive oil

Directions:

1. Put the water in your instant pot, add salt and the baking soda, and the steamer basket, add celeriac fries inside, cover, cook on High for 4 minutes, drain and transfer them to a bowl.
2. Place olive oil on a pan and heat over medium high heat, add celeriac fries, cook until they are gold on all sides, drain grease, transfer them to plates and serve as a side dish.
3. Enjoy!

Nutritional Info: 182 Calories, 5g Fat, 7g Carbs, 10g Protein

Carrots with Thyme and Dill

Servings: 4

Ingredients:

- ½ c. water
- 1 lb. baby carrots
- 3 tbsps. stevia
- 1 tbsp. chopped thyme
- 1 tbsp. chopped dill
- Salt
- 2 tbsps. ghee

Directions:

1. Put the water in your instant pot, add the steamer basket, add carrots inside, cover, cook on High for 3 minutes, drain and transfer to a bowl.
2. Set your instant pot on Sauté mode, add ghee, melt it, add stevia, thyme, dill and return carrots as well.
3. Stir, cook for a couple of minutes, divide between plates and serve as a side dish.
4. Enjoy!

Nutritional Info: 162 Calories, 4g Fat, 8g Carbs, 3g Protein

Desserts

Chocolate Cream

Servings: 4

Ingredients:

- 2 c. Heavy cream
- ¼ c. Chopped dark chocolate
- 3 Eggs
- 1 tsp. Orange zest
- 1 tsp. Stevia powder
- 1 tsp. Vanilla extract
- ½ tsp. Salt

Directions:

1. Plug in your instant pot and press the 'Saute' button. Add heavy cream, chopped chocolate, stevia powder, vanilla extract, orange zest, and salt. Stir well and simmer until the chocolate has completely melted. Press the 'Cancel' button and crack eggs, one at the time, stirring constantly. Remove from the instant pot.
2. Transfer the mixture to 4 mason jars with loose lids.
3. Pour 2 cups of water in your instant pot and set the trivet in the stainless steel insert. Add jars and seal the lid.
4. Set the steam release handle and press the 'Manual' button. Set the timer for 10 minutes.
5. When done, perform a quick release by moving the steam valve to the 'Venting' position.
6. Open the lid and remove the jars. Chill to a room temperature and then transfer to the refrigerator.
7. Top with some whipped cream before serving.

Nutritional Info:267 Calories, 26.2g Fat, 2.4g Carbs, 5.6g Protein

Butter Pancakes

Servings: 6

Ingredients:

- 2 c. Cream cheese
- 2 c. Almond flour
- 6 Large eggs
- ¼ tsp. Salt
- 2 tbsps. Butter
- ¼ tsp. Ground ginger
- ½ tsp. Cinnamon powder

Directions:

1. In a mixing bowl, mix eggs, cream cheese, and one tablespoon of butter. With a paddle attachment on, beat well on high speed until light and creamy. Slowly add flour beating constantly. Finally, add salt, ginger, and cinnamon. Continue to beat until fully incorporated.
2. Plug in your instant pot and press the 'Saute' button. Grease the stainless steel insert with the remaining butter and heat up.
3. Pour in about ½ cup of the batter and cook for 2-3 minutes or until golden color. Repeat the process with the remaining batter.
4. Serve warm.

Nutritional Info:432 Calories, 40.2g Fat, 3.5g Carbs, 14g Protein

Instant Pot Eggnog

Servings: 4

Ingredients:

- 3 c. Almond milk
- 10 Egg yolks
- 1 c. Swerve
- 3 c. Whipped cream
- 1 tsp. Vanilla extract
- 2 tsps. Rum extract
- ½ tsp. Ground cinnamon

Directions:

1. Plug in your instant pot and press the 'Saute' button. Add unsweetened almond milk, vanilla extract, and cinnamon. Stir well and cook for 5-6 minutes.
2. Meanwhile, place egg yolks in a deep bowl. Add one cup of swerve and stir well. Pour the mixture into the instant pot and mix well.
3. Continue to cook for another 2 minutes.
4. Finally, stir in whipped cream and rum extract. Gently simmer for 2-3 minutes and press the 'Cancel' button.
5. Transfer the eggnog to serving glasses and chill to a room temperature.
6. Refrigerate for 1 hour before serving.

Nutritional Info:437 Calories, 41.7g Fat, 5.3g Carbs, 9.5g Protein

Pumpkin Pie Pancakes

Servings: 4

Ingredients:

- 1 c. Pumpkin puree
- 3 Large eggs
- 2 tbsps. Swerve
- ¾ c. Almond flour
- 4 tbsps. Unsweetened almond milk
- 1 tsp. Pumpkin pie seasoning
- ¼ tsp. Salt
- 2 tbsps. Baking powder

Directions:

1. In a mixing bowl, mix pumpkin pie seasoning, eggs, swerve, and almond milk. With a whisking attachment on, beat well on high speed. Gradually add flour, salt, baking powder, and pumpkin pie seasoning. Continue to mix for another 2 minutes.
2. Finally, add the pumpkin puree and mix well again.
3. Plug in your instant pot and press the 'Saute' button. Grease the stainless steel insert with some oil and heat up. Add about ¼ cup of the batter and cook for 3 minutes.
4. When done, gently remove from your instant pot and top with some blueberries, raspberries, or almonds.

Nutritional Info:143 Calories, 10g Fat, 5.7g Carbs, 6.9g Protein

Coconut Brownies with Raspberries

Servings: 6

Ingredients:

- 1½ c. Almond flour
- ½ c. Raspberries
- ½ c. Shredded coconut
- ¼ c. Swerve
- 1 tsp. Baking soda
- ½ c. Coconut oil
- 2 Large eggs

Directions:

1. Combine together almond flour, shredded coconut, baking soda, and swerve. Mix well and add coconut oil and eggs. With a dough hook attachment, beat well until completely combined. Fold in raspberries and set aside.
2. Line a small baking pan with some parchment paper and add the mixture. Press well with your hands and tightly wrap with aluminum foil.
3. Plug in your instant pot and pour in 1 cup of water. Set the trivet and place the baking pan on top.
4. Seal the lid and set the steam release handle. Press the 'Manual' button and set the timer for 20 minutes.
5. When you hear the cooker's end signal, perform a quick release and open the lid.
6. Remove the baking pan and cool completely before slicing.
7. Optionally, sprinkle with some more shredded coconut.

Nutritional Info:251 Calories, 25.5g Fat, 1.9g Carbs, 4g Protein

Vanilla Cream

Servings: 4

Ingredients:

- 8 Large eggs
- ¾ c. Unsweetened almond milk
- 1½ c. Heavy cream
- 1 tsp. Vanilla extract, sliced and seeded
- 1 Vanilla bean
- 4 tbsps. Swerve

Directions:

1. Place vanilla extract in a mixing bowl along with the remaining ingredients.
2. With a whisking attachment on, beat the mixture for 2 minutes on high speed and transfer into 4 ramekins. Tightly wrap with aluminum foil and set aside.
3. Plug in your instant pot and pour in 2 cups of water. Set the trivet at the bottom of the stainless steel insert and carefully place the ramekins on top.
4. Seal the lid and set the steam release handle to the 'Sealing' position. Press the 'Manual' button and set the timer for 15 minutes.
5. When done, perform a quick release by moving the pressure valve to the 'Venting' position.
6. Open the lid and carefully remove the ramekins from your instant pot.
7. Cool to a room temperature without removing the aluminum foil.
8. Transfer to the fridge and cool completely before serving.

Nutritional Info:309 Calories, 27.3g Fat, 2.3g Carbs, 13.7g Protein

Cherry Pudding

Servings: 5

Ingredients:

- ¾ c. Whipped cream
- ¾ c. Unsweetened almond milk
- 4 Egg whites
- 3 tsps. Powdered stevia
- 1 tsp. Sugar-free cherry extract
- ¼ tsp. Xanthan gum

Directions:

1. In a mixing bowl, mix almond milk, heavy cream, and egg whites. Beat well on high, for 3 minutes. Pour the mixture into 5 ramekins.
2. Plug in your instant pot and pour 2 cups of water into the stainless steel insert. Position a trivet at the bottom and place the ramekins on top. Securely lock the lid and adjust the steam release handle. Press "Manual" button and set the timer for 3 minutes. Cook on high pressure.
3. When you hear the cooker's end signal, press "Cancel" button and release the pressure naturally.
4. Open the pot and chill the pudding to a room temperature. Refrigerate for 1 hour before serving.

Nutritional Info:153 Calories, 14g Fat, 2g Carbs, 4.5g Protein

Chocolate Mousse

Servings: 5

Ingredients:

- 4 egg yolks
- ¼ c. water
- ¼ c. cacao
- ½ c. swerve
- 1 c. whipping cream
- ½ tsp. vanilla
- ½ c. almond milk
- sea salt

Directions:
1. Whisk the eggs.
2. Combine the water, swerve, and cacao in a saucepan until well mixed.
3. Stir in the milk and cream. Warm up – to just boiling – and turn off the heat.
4. Measure about one tablespoon of the chocolate mixture into dish with the eggs. Whisk and slowly empty the rest of the chocolate into the mix.
5. Empty the mousse into 5 jars/ramekins.
6. Pour 1 ½ cups of water into the Instant Pot. Add the trivet and place the jars into the pot.
7. Secure the top and set the timer for six minutes.
8. Quick release the pressure and remove the jars with some tongs.
9. Let them cool before placing them in the fridge four to six hours.

Nutritional Info: 251 Calories, 23.3g Fat, 4.4g Carbs, 5.6g Protein

ocolate Peanut Butter Cheesecake

Servings: 8

Ingredients:

- 2 large eggs
- 16 oz. cheese
- 2 tbsps. peanut butter, powdered
- 1 tsp. vanilla extract
- 1 tbsp. cocoa
- ½ c. sugar substitute (your choice)

Directions:

1. Let all of the fixings come to room temperature. Toss the eggs and cream cheese into the blender. Mix until smooth.
2. Add the remainder of the components and blend well.
3. Add the mixture into 4 (4 oz.) mason jars and cover with some aluminum foil or jar lid.
4. Pour one cup of water into the Instant Pot. You will need to prepare in two batches.
5. Cook on the high setting for 15 to 18 minutes. Natural release and chill overnight or at least several hours.

Nutritional Info: 191 Calories, 16g Fat, 5g Carbs, 6g Protein

Coconut Cake

Servings: 8

Ingredients:

- 1 c. almond flour
- ½ c. shredded coconut, unsweetened
- 1/3 c. Truvia
- 1 tsp. Apple pie spice
- 1 tsp. Baking powder

Wet Ingredients

- ¼ c. melted butter
- 2 eggs, lightly whisked
- ½ c. heavy whipping cream

Directions:

1. Combine all of the dry fixings. Add each of the 'wet' ingredients – one at a time.
2. Empty the batter into the pan, and cover with foil.
3. Empty the water into the Instant Pot, and place the steamer rack.
4. Set the timer 40 minutes using the high-pressure setting. Natural release for ten minutes. Then, quick release.
5. Remove the pan and let it cool 15 to 20 minutes. Flip it over onto a platter and garnish as desired (count the carbs).

Nutritional Info:
236 Calories, 23g Fat, 3g Carbs, 5g Protein

Lemon Ricotta Cheesecake

Servings: 6

Ingredients:

- 8 oz. cream cheese
- ¼ c. Truvia
- lemon – the Zest and juice
- 1/3 c. Ricotta cheese
- ½ tsp. lemon extract
- 2 eggs

Topping Ingredients

- 1 tsp. Truvia
- 1 tbsp. sour cream

Directions:

1. Combine all of the fixings in a stand mixer (omit the eggs).
2. Taste test and add the eggs. Use the low speed, since over-beating the eggs will cause the crust to crack.
3. Add the batter to the pan. Cover with foil/silicone lid.
4. Add the trivet and two cups of water and arrange the pan in the Instant Pot.
5. Cook 30 minutes (high-pressure). Natural release the pressure.
6. Blend in the sweetener of choice and sour cream. Decorate the warm cake and place in the fridge to chill for six to eight hours.

Nutritional Info: 278 Calories, 19.2g Fat, 6.1g Carbs, 18.8g Protein

Cacao Avocado Cake

Servings: 3

Ingredients:

- ¼ c. avocado, mashed
- 1 ripe banana
- ½ c. cocoa powder
- ½ tsp. apple cider vinegar
- 3 tbsps. coconut oil, melted
- 2 tbsps. sweetener (your choice)
- ¾ tsp. baking soda
- 2 tsps. fresh lemon juice
- 1 c. water

Directions:

1. Blend all ingredients in a blender.
2. Lightly grease three mini ramekins with coconut oil. Pour the batter into ramekins until they are about 3 of the way full.
3. Pour the water into your Instant Pot and add the steaming rack. Place the pans onto the steaming rack.
4. Close and lock the lid. Press MANUAL for high pressure and set cooking time to 18 minutes.
5. Use the quick release the pressure by flipping the valve on the lid.
6. Serve warm or cold.

Nutritional Info: 349.7 Calories, 30.9g Fat, 11.7g Carbs, 3.5g Protein

Raspberry Compote

Servings: 4

Ingredients:

- 2 c. Raspberries
- 1 c. Swerve
- 1 tsp. Grated lemon zest
- 1 tsp. Vanilla extract

Directions:

1. Plug in your instant pot and press the 'Saute' button. Add raspberries, swerve, lemon zest, and vanilla extract. Stir well and pour in 1 cup of water. Cook for 5 minutes, stirring constantly.
2. Now pour in 2 more cups of water and press the 'Cancel' button. Seal the lid and set the steam release handle to the 'Sealing' position. Press the 'Manual' button and set the timer for 15 minutes on low pressure.
3. When you hear the cooker's end signal, press the 'Cancel' button and release the pressure naturally for 10-15 minutes. Move the pressure handle to the 'Venting' position to release any remaining pressure and open the lid.
4. Optionally, stir some more lemon juice and transfer to serving bowls.
5. Chill to a room temperature and refrigerate for one hour before serving.

Nutritional Info:48 Calories, 0.5g Fat, 5g Carbs, 1g Protein

Conclusion

I hope this guide has helped you to understand and embrace the benefits of the Instant Pot in Ketogenic Diets. Once you have grown accustomed to how the diet works, and the recipes in this book, venture out and discover the endless assortment of Ketogenic-friendly recipes, or even make a few of your own.
Happy cooking!

Peter Bragg

Made in the USA
Lexington, KY
26 October 2018